Sharpen Your Writing Skills

SHARPEN YOUR
Essay
Writing Skills

Jennifer Rozines Roy
Johannah Haney

Enslow Publishers, Inc.
40 Industrial Road
Box 398
Berkeley Heights, NJ 07922
USA

http://www.enslow.com

Original edition published as *You Can Write an Essay* in 2004.

Library of Congress Cataloging-in-Publication Data

Roy, Jennifer Rozines, 1967–
    Sharpen Your Essay Writing Skills / Jennifer Rozines Roy and Johannah Haney.
        p. cm. — (Sharpen your writing skills)
    Includes index.
    Summary: "Find out about the different kinds of essays, how to write an essay, making your essay better, presenting your essay, and a sample student essay"—Provided by publisher.
    ISBN 978-0-7660-3903-2
    1. English language—Composition and exercises—Study and teaching (Elementary)—Juvenile literature. 2. Essay—Authorship—Problems, exercises, etc.—Juvenile literature. I. Haney, Johannah. II. Title.
    LB1576.R76 2011
    808.4—dc22
    2010053474

Paperback ISBN: 978-1-59845-342-3

Printed in China

052011 Leo Paper Group, Heshan City, Guangdong, China

10 9 8 7 6 5 4 3 2 1

Illustration Credits: Enslow Publishers, Inc.

Cover Illustration: Shutterstock.com

Table of Contents

1 You Can Write an Essay 5

2 All About Essays 10

3 Before You Write 26

4 Time to Write! 40

5 Making It Even Better 46

6 Presenting It 52

A Sample Student Essay 57

Glossary 61

*Further Reading and
Internet Addresses* 63

Index 64

Chapter One

You Can Write an Essay

"Write an essay . . ."

These are three words that you are likely to see over and over—at school during an in-class assignment or standardized test, at home for a take-home assignment, on a college application, perhaps even at your job.

When you think of essays, what is your first reaction?

(a) "Hurray! I get to write an essay!"

or

(b) "Oh no, I have to write an essay ..."

or even

(c) "What the heck is an essay, and how do I write one?"

E-S-S-A-Y!
You can do it if you try!

If you answered "Hurray," good for you! You've already learned that essays are an effective and interesting way to express yourself. This book will give you even more information and ideas about how to write good essays.

If your answer was (b) or (c), don't worry. Help is on the way. In this book, you will learn the steps of writing an essay and what makes a good essay—and how to have fun doing it. So, when you get an assignment that says, "Write an essay . . . ," instead of thinking "No way," you'll say "Hurray!"

What Is an Essay?

An essay is a piece of writing that deals with one main subject. It can be as short as couple of paragraphs or as long as a few pages. An essay contains information about that subject and presents it in an organized, interesting way. An essay has a beginning, a middle, and an end. It contains a thesis statement, which is the idea that holds the whole essay together.

Essays can be answers to test questions. They can also be compositions in which the writer expresses his or her opinions or tries to make certain points.

While their purposes may differ, all essays spotlight a central topic.

Effective essays contain solid facts that support the main subject. That means you can't just write a lot of "stuff" down to fill a page. A good essay requires research and planning, thinking and judging. When you're writing an essay, you need to show that you are credible—that means you can be trusted and you know what you're talking about.

So, what are essays about? Almost anything in the world! From entertainment to science, current events to adventures, school to family . . . well, you get the point. Here are some examples of essay questions,

Essays can:
- ✔ **inform**—share knowledge about a subject
- ✔ **explain**—make a concept or idea clearer
- ✔ **analyze**—examine a topic in depth, part by part
- ✔ **persuade**—convince or win over another person; make others take your side on an issue
- ✔ **inspire**—get people excited about something or cause people to feel strong emotions

or prompts (statements that tell you what to write about):

1. Describe a funny event in your life. What was so funny about it? What do you remember most about that event?

2. Write a review of your favorite poem. Why do you think it is the best poem ever written? What would you tell your friends about it to convince them that they should read it?

3. Explain how to conduct a science experiment. Include details that will allow the reader to copy your experiment.

4. Compare the campaigns of two presidential candidates before an election. What makes them different?

5. Evaluate a rule at your school. Does the rule make school better? Worse? How so?

Why Learn How to Write an Essay?

One reason to know how to write an essay is obvious—good grades. A good essay shows your teacher that you have a good understanding of a subject. It proves that you were paying attention in class and that you studied and did your homework. An essay allows you to express yourself in a more thorough way than just answering a multiple choice or true-false question does, and it proves that you can put information together to support a viewpoint.

You'll also probably need to write at least one essay (often two or three) to get into college. Colleges want to know more about you than just the basic facts. Essays can give them a better sense of who you are and help them determine whether you would be a good fit for their school. They can also show how logically, creatively, and clearly you think and how well you express yourself in writing.

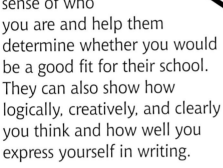

These are really solid!

Even beyond school, essays are a popular way for writers to express themselves. You probably have seen essays in newspapers, magazines, or books. Columnists write essays on subjects they are curious about or interested in. Reviewers write essays to voice their opinions about places or events. Anyone can write an essay and try to get it published. You don't have to be a professional writer. You just need a subject, your knowledge of essay writing, and your own unique style of expressing your ideas.

When you write an effective essay, you have an audience that is waiting to learn about a subject from you. Writing an essay is a chance for you to express your unique thoughts and opinions. You have the power to teach others, change people's minds, and inspire action. So, let's get started!

All About Essays

There are three main types of essays: *narrative*, *persuasive*, and *expository*. Narrative essays are about a personal experience you have had. Persuasive essays aim to convince your readers to believe the same thing you do about a subject. Expository essays explain something in detail.

Time to learn all about each type of essay.

Narrative Essays

A narrative essay tells a true story. In this type of essay, the writer shares an experience that happened in real life in the form of a story. This gives the writer a chance to write about something meaningful, unusual, or funny. You can write a narrative essay about your memory of a person, event, or moment.

Every narrative essay has a main point. The main point is the most important thought or lesson that you are writing about. For example, pretend you are writing an essay about saving money to buy the new game you wanted. You might describe why you wanted the game, how you earned and saved money to buy it, and the way you felt when you handed the cashier at the store your money and got your game in return. The main point of your essay might be that saving money is hard work, but it pays off when you reach your goal. You might state this point directly in your essay or let the outcome speak for itself.

Persuasive Essays

A persuasive essay aims to convince your audience to agree with your opinions on a subject, or it aims to inspire action by presenting a well-developed argument that includes facts and opinions.

Hey, I have a main point too!

Every issue has at least two sides. When writing a persuasive essay, you are presenting your opinions on one side of the issue. For instance, consider the issue of skateboarding in public areas.

A person can take one of several different positions on this issue. For example:

1. Skateboarding should be allowed in all public areas.
2. Skateboarding should be allowed only in certain public areas.
3. Skateboarding should not be allowed in any public areas.

No matter which side of an argument you take in a persuasive essay, you must find facts and use them to support your opinion. By doing so, you show your audience that you have thought carefully about your ideas.

To build your strongest case, it is important to consider the other side of the issue. Think about what facts would be used to support another point of view and how you would counter those facts with your own. This approach will help you to understand your own position better and show how carefully you've weighed the facts. You will then be more likely to win over your audience, which is what persuasion is all about.

There are two types of persuasive essays: a *problem/solution* persuasive essay and a *position paper*. Each of these types has a different purpose.

Problem/Solution Essays

A problem/solution persuasive essay presents a problem and argues for a specific solution to it. When you are writing a problem/solution paper, you must first clearly state what the problem is. Then you should offer a way this problem could be solved. In your essay, you will use facts and evidence to show why the solution you are proposing would correct the problem.

For example, perhaps you have noticed that not many students in your school know when and where extracurricular activities take place. Maybe the last few softball games haven't filled the bleachers, or there was confusion over where play tryouts were going to be held. You could write a problem/solution essay. In this essay, you first must show that students do not know enough about what is going on in their school. You might do some of your own research by asking students to try to name what events are taking place at school in the next week; you could then use the results as evidence. In your essay, you could suggest solutions like starting a school newsletter to pass out to students, adding school activities to the daily announcements, or setting up a bulletin board outside the cafeteria that lists upcoming events.

Position Papers

A position paper states your position on an issue and gives details to support your views. It is important to use evidence to support your opinion. Suppose you are writing an essay saying that all school buses should install seat belts that students are required to wear. First you might show that seat belts can help prevent people from getting hurt in car accidents. You might also find evidence in newspaper or magazine articles that shows that students have been injured in school bus accidents. Perhaps you can even find evidence that schools that do use seat belts have fewer problems with misbehavior because students cannot stand up or move around while the bus is moving. It is not enough to just say, "Schools should put seat belts in buses and make students wear them." You must present genuine facts to try to convince your audience to agree with you.

Expository Essays

Expository essays explain things. The word "expository" comes from "expose." When you expose something, you show what it really is, like showing a celebrity without his or her makeup. Different types of expository essays expose different things. An expository essay can show how two things are the same or how they are different. It can explain how one event causes another to happen. Expository essays can also describe a process. Like the other types of essays, expository essays use facts to illustrate the main point.

There are three main types of expository essays: *process papers*, *compare-and-contrast essays*, and *cause-and-effect essays*.

Process Papers

A process paper explains how to make something, how to do a specific task, or how something works. Process papers are very detailed. A process paper is like a magnifying glass or microscope, showing the smallest details. For example, you could write a process paper on something simple, like how to clean your room quickly when a relative drops by for an unexpected visit. Let's look at an example:

First, pick up all the clothes on the floor and toss them in the hamper or a box. Next make your bed; you can just arrange the top cover neatly with the sheets underneath still rumpled. Throw away anything that is trash. Then gather all the junk lying around and find a spot (like under the bed or in a box in the closet) to store it until you can go through it when you have more time. After that, gather loose papers and stack them neatly on your desk. If there's time, dust quickly with a wet paper towel.

Other possible topics for process papers might include how paper is made, how to cook your favorite meal, or how bicycles work.

Compare-and-Contrast Essay

This kind of essay explores the ways two or more things are the same and the ways they are different. When you compare, you will write about the similarities. When you contrast, you will write about the differences. An essay question or prompt might ask you only to compare, or only to contrast, or to do both. Let's look at some examples:

1. Compare and contrast the way your parents treat you now with the way they treated you when you were younger.

To answer this essay question, you would show both the ways that your parents treat you differently now and the ways that your parents treat you the same

A process paper lets you look up close at the smallest parts of something.

now. You might say you have more responsibilities with housework now, but you also enjoy more privileges, like having sleepovers and riding bikes with your friends in the neighborhood. You might also say that just as when you were younger, you have to follow the family rules, such as letting your parents know where you are at all times and doing homework before you watch TV.

2. Compare your two favorite seasons. What do you like about each of them? Why?

To answer this essay question, you would pick your two favorite seasons and show the good qualities they have in common. You might choose spring and fall, because you like that both seasons have cool temperatures. Or, you might choose spring and summer because you can play outside more often during these months. You could also choose summer and winter, and show that both have fun holidays to celebrate, like New Year's Eve and Independence Day.

3. Contrast the feeling you get from reading a book and the feeling you get from watching a movie.

In this essay, you would write about the ways reading and watching movies affect you in different ways. You might say that you enjoy reading stories so you can let your imagination draw the characters and setting in your mind. When you watch a movie, however, the setting and characters are right before your eyes, so maybe you enjoy being able to focus on other details in movies.

Cause-and-Effect Essays

Cause-and-effect essays show how one action causes another action. They discuss cause-and-effect relationships. What is a cause-and-effect relationship? For example, eating too much junk food can lead to weight gain and health problems. The cause is eating too much junk food, and the effect is weight gain and health problems.

A cause-and-effect essay uses facts to prove that a certain cause produces a certain effect. Pretend you

Oops!

are writing a cause-and-effect essay about exercising. You could use facts to show that exercising has positive effects on muscles and strength. Other possible topics include the effects of pollution on the environment, the effects of rain on flowers and plants, or the effects the Internet has on how people learn.

Now that you know about the different types of essays you might be asked to write, let's take a look at when you will be asked to write them.

A cause-and-effect essay shows how one thing causes another.

Writing Essays for Different Purposes

You will be asked to write essays in many different circumstances. Your teacher might give a take-home assignment, where you can do research on your own time and craft your essay at home over several days. An essay might also appear in an exam, where you must draw on your knowledge of the subject and write your essay immediately during the test period. You might have to write an in-class essay about the issues you are discussing in a social studies class. If you plan to go to college, you may also have to write one or more essays on the application forms. Essays allow college admissions officers—the people who decide who gets accepted into their school—the chance to see your writing, thinking, and reasoning skills, and to get to know you better. There are strategies you can use during each of these situations that will help you to write a successful essay.

Writing Essays at School

There are two main circumstances under which you will write an essay at school: in-class essays, and essays on a test. An *in-class essay* requires you to write about a subject in a limited time frame at your desk. An *essay test* examines how well you know a subject you have been studying. It can also test how well you write or how well you analyze material from a short reading section. A test might be made up entirely of essays, or you might have to write an essay along with answering multiple choice, true-false, and short-answer questions.

Another type of in-class essay might appear on a *standardized test.* Standardized tests are used to see how well students are doing within a particular school district, city, and state. These tests are not graded by your teacher, but by an outside evaluator. Standardized tests do not count toward your grades, but they might affect what classes you are placed in or whether you can go on to the next grade level. When you are in high school, you may take the SATs. Many colleges look at the scores on these standardized tests as part of the admission process.

Standardized tests used to just involve filling in bubbles with a number-two pencil. But now, some standardized tests also require students to write an essay. The SAT includes an essay section.

Doing well on an in-class essay or essay test requires more than just being able to "recycle" memorized information to your teacher. You need to be able to understand how different ideas and facts work together. You then must show what you have learned and express it in writing.

The first step is to make sure you understand the essay question. What will your teacher or other evaluator be looking for? Look for key verbs such as *describe*, *explain*, *compare*, *contrast*, and *prove* to determine the essay's purpose. Next, spend a little time thinking about your knowledge of the subject. What facts and ideas did you learn in class? From homework? During time you spent studying for the test or preparing for the in-class essay?

When you write essays at school, you have only a certain amount of time to write. It is important to make the very best use of your time. If an essay question appears on a test that also contains multiple choice, true-false, short-answer, and matching questions, you must spend enough time on those questions as well as on your essay. And you might have more than one essay to write during the test period. It might sound scary at first, but there are lots of things you can do to make it go smoothly.

An essay question might ask you to pick a side of an argument to prove. Keep in mind that there is usually not one "right" answer. The teacher or evaluator wants to see how well you support whichever position you choose.

If you have five minutes to write your essay, you should spend only a few moments deciding what to write about. If you have twenty minutes to write your essay, you can spend a couple of minutes deciding. If you are having a hard time making a decision about what to write, just pick a subject that you think you can write about and go for it.

First, use a piece of scrap paper to jot down notes or make an outline. Refer to these notes while you are writing, and you'll be less likely to leave something out.

Now it's time to start writing! Begin with a point that you feel is important to get your essay off to a strong start. Then—keep going.

If you get stuck looking for the perfect word, just try to pick one that is good enough and keep writing. You might have time to go back and think of the best words later, but you will get more credit for your ideas than for your vocabulary. If you start running out of time, outline the ideas that you planned to use in the last part of the essay. Your teacher will be able to see your thought process and you might get more credit. Double-check to make sure that your essay responds to the question.

Depending on the essay question, essays that you write in class might be one paragraph long, or they might need a few paragraphs. If you feel you can answer the question fully in one paragraph, you will introduce what you are trying to prove in your

Writing on the fly:

Writing an essay in class can be stressful. Remember these tips to do the best job possible on your essay:

- ✔ Stay calm.
- ✔ Prepare in advance by studying.
- ✔ Read the essay prompt carefully.
- ✔ Make an outline.
- ✔ Remain focused.
- ✔ Read your essay when you are finished.
- ✔ Make sure you answered the question.

first sentence. The middle sentences will provide the information that supports your main point. The last sentence will summarize your essay. More complex essay questions might need to be answered in several paragraphs. The first paragraph will introduce the subject and say what you are trying to prove. The middle paragraph(s) will include the details and facts that support your main idea. The last paragraph will summarize your essay.

One of the best things you can do when you write an essay at school is to remain calm. Remember: After reading this book, you will know how to write a good essay. Writing essays at school will give you the opportunity to show your teacher just how well you know your subject.

Let's look at an example of an essay prompt and response written in class.

Essay Prompt: Describe two ways the events of September 11, 2001, have affected the United States.

The events of September 11, 2001, have affected the United States in many ways. The attacks made us realize we were not as prepared as we thought. As a result, better methods of security have been put in place to prevent future attacks. Another way the events of September 11, 2001 have impacted the U.S. is that we are more aware of how other countries see us. We have a better understanding of what effects our decisions have on other countries.

Take-Home Essays

Take-home essays provide a little more "breathing room," because you have several days to choose a topic, do research, and write your essay. It is important to plan your time well when writing a take-home essay. Remember that you must do research, write an outline, compose and edit a rough draft, and prepare a final draft. (Of course, not all essays require research—for instance, for a narrative essay, the information may all come from the writer's mind—yours!)

When planning your time, make sure to account for difficulties that will likely come up—the book you need may not be in the library, your computer may crash, your little sister or brother might spill juice all over your papers. Be well prepared!

Because you have more time to prepare takehome essays, your teacher will want to see that you have thought through your ideas, have considered word choice carefully, and have made an effort to make your essay mistake-free. Read your essay out loud, to another person, or to yourself. Listen for words or phrases that sound out of place or repetitious.

College Application Essays

It's never too soon to start thinking about it! When you apply to colleges and universities, you may be asked to write an essay to go along with your other application materials. Writing an essay for college allows the admissions officers to learn more about you and decide whether you would make a good student at their school. For the most part, different colleges will use different essay questions. They are all designed to allow you to show how you think, what you find important, what motivates you—and, of course, how well you can write. Let's look at some sample college application essay questions:

1. If you could interview any historical figure, whom would you interview? Why did you choose that person? What would you ask him or her?

2. Describe the most important moment in your life. What did you learn from it?

3. What work of art, literature, or science has inspired you? How so?

When you write any essay, especially a college application essay, you want to make your essay stand out and reflect who you really are. One way to do this is to say something surprising. For example, if you are answering question 3 above, you might say that the work of literature that has inspired you is Dr. Seuss's *Green Eggs and Ham.* This would be surprising, because other students are probably choosing books they read in high school. You might say that *Green Eggs and Ham* helped you realize that you must try new things, even things you think you might not like, in order to grow as a person. If you are applying to a college away from home, for example, you could say that the book has helped you realize that taking a risk on leaving the comfort of your hometown is important to your becoming more independent.

I'm applying to Pencil State University to major in writing. I'd better get started on my essay!

Now that you know about the types of essays and the different situations in which they are written, it's time to learn about the steps you'll take to write them.

Chapter Three

Before You Write

Before you sit down and start writing away, there are a few things you must do to prepare for your essay.

1. Choose your topic.

2. Depending on the type of essay, do your research or think about the information you'll need to include.

3. Organize your information in a graphic organizer such as an outline.

4. Write a rough draft.

5. Revise, edit, and proofread.

6. Prepare the final draft.

You'll learn about these steps in the chapters to come. Let's get started!

Step #1: Know or Choose Your Topic

The subject of your essay is called the topic. When you receive an essay assignment, the first thing that you need to do is find out what your topic is. Your teacher might assign one topic that you must write about, give you a few topics from which to choose, or allow you to choose your own topic within a broader set of guidelines.

Essay Prompts

When you are assigned an essay topic, the assignment usually is in the form of a question or prompt. For example, an essay question might read, "How has the way people communicate changed in the past twenty years?" An essay prompt might read, "Discuss the changes over the past twenty years in the ways people communicate." Reading the essay question carefully can give you some important clues about what you should write about in your essay. Here are a few of the clue words you might see in an essay prompt that help you "decode" what it is really asking you to do:

- **Compare/contrast**—Write about the ways two or more things are the same and the ways they are different.

- **Analyze**—Break down a topic into smaller pieces and look at the topic in depth.

- **Describe or explain**—Write about the topic in detail. Focus your essay on meaningful aspects of the topic.

- **Evaluate**—Tell how well something (such as a rule or project) works.
- **Cause and effect**—Show how one action (the cause) makes the other thing (the effect) happen.

How to Choose a Topic

Choosing a topic is a very important step in the writing process. You will enjoy writing your essay most if you have a topic that appeals to you. If you are given a broad choice of topics, it will probably be easy for you to find something that excites you. What are your interests? What would you like people to know about?

But what if your teacher assigns the topic for your essay and you don't think it's interesting? Often you can find an intriguing aspect to a topic that you don't think is thrilling at first glance.

Be an essay detective—read the question or prompt carefully to look for clues about what you should write.

Can I help?

For example, say your teacher assigns you an essay about methods of communication. Maybe you have never thought much about the ways people communicate. Try to find an aspect of communication that interests you. Do you like computers? You could write an essay about how e-mail and instant messaging have changed the way people exchange information. Are you a history buff? Write an essay about Alexander Graham Bell, the man who invented the telephone. Are you a sports fan? Think about writing an essay about how athletic teams communicate on the playing field without letting their opponents know what they are saying.

In some cases, you might not be able to decide on a topic right away. Or you might need to choose between two or more topics that you are interested in writing about. Do some exploring. Type your choices into a search engine on the Internet and see what information comes up. Is there enough material on the topic? Does what you see really interest you? Another method that might help is to check the online catalog at the library or skim the Table of Contents and Index sections of books on your topics. You might find that one of your topics seems like a good choice at first, but the research material is hard to find, or the research material available on one of your choices might be more interesting and fun to read than that on the other topics.

When you choose your topic, make sure that it is broad enough that you will be able to find lots of research materials. On the other hand, make sure it is not too broad. For example, you will find lots of research material about astronomy, but you must choose one small part of astronomy, such as "black holes" or "Saturn's rings," so your topic can be detailed.

Thesis Statements

All essays should contain a *thesis statement*. Think of it as THE idea that holds the entire essay together. A thesis statement is the sentence in your essay that tells the reader exactly what your essay is about. It usually comes in the first paragraph. All of your research and writing will deal directly with the thesis statement. It usually includes two or three main points that you will prove in your essay.

One good way to decide what your thesis statement will be is to ask a key question about your topic. Limit your response to two or three brief reasons. Let's look at an example. Your topic is technology. You want to show the ways in which technology has improved the world. Ask yourself,

How has technology improved the world?

It has given people a better life by . . .

- improving medical care
- adding convenience
- increasing jobs

As you think about your responses to your question, look for ways to pinpoint your thesis statement further. In the above example, a strong thesis would be, "Technology has given people a better life by improving medical care, adding convenience, and increasing jobs." Notice that the thesis does not include the original question like the first example did. The responses to this question uncovered an opportunity to make the thesis more exact: Technology makes people's lives better.

For take-home essays, when you think you have your thesis statement written, run it by your teacher, parents, or classmates and ask for feedback. Knowing your thesis statement is good and solid will make your research and writing go more smoothly. While doing your research, you might find information that makes you think differently about your topic than you did before.

Step #2: Research

For in-class essays and essays on tests, the research you will do is called STUDYING. Reviewing your textbooks, class material, notes, handouts, and homework are all excellent ways to study for in-class and test question essays.

Take-home essays, however, often require research from sources outside your class material. Once you have decided on a thesis statement, it is time to gather facts on your topic. The first thing to do is find sources for your research, such as books, periodicals (like magazines and newspapers), and Web sites. Let's look at the different ways to do research.

Library

The library is one of the best places to start when you are doing research for any project, including essays.

There are many resources available to you at a library, including books, periodicals, Internet access, and a staff of librarians to help you find it all. When you are searching for your topic, remember to try different kinds of words in your search. For example, if you are writing about figure skating, you might look up "figure skating," "Winter Olympics," and the names of your favorite skaters to find good research material.

Internet

The Internet is a great place to find research material, but you must be careful about what kind of Web site your information comes from. For instance, if you are writing an essay on the harmful effects of cigarette smoking, you probably would not want to use information from the Web sites of companies that make tobacco products. Better Web sites to visit would be those of the Centers for Disease Control, the American Heart Association, or another health-related organization that will present reliable and factual information.

When you search the library directory, you search in the card catalog at the library or on the Internet, you will probably get more results than you need. You must decide which of these sources will work for your essay. One of the best ways to find the right book sources for your essay is to look in the Table of Contents and Index sections of books. You will see at a glance whether the book will be helpful to your research. Many Internet sites have links on the homepage that will show you the topics covered within the Web site. Use these links like a table of contents in a

How do I know who is behind a Web site? Here are some examples:

.com—Anyone can have a Web site with a .com address, so be extremely cautious about information you gather from these sites.

.org—This is a Web site run by a nonprofit organization. Many of these sites offer reliable information. But keep in mind that they are also presenting the point of view of the organization.

.edu—This is a Web site run by an educational institution, such as a college or university. These Web sites usually provide reliable information.

.gov—This is a Web site run by an official government organization. These Web sites provide very reliable information.

book—glance through them and decide if the Web site will help your research. You can also find more sources by checking the references in articles and on Web sites (and you can often evaluate articles by checking their sources).

When you decide which research materials you want to use, remember that you don't have to read them all cover to cover. You might find a book about the great inventors, but your essay is going to focus on one specific inventor. Even if you have a book all about the inventor you are writing about, you might be able to just read the section that deals with your main point.

Step #3: Taking Notes

Once you have chosen good sources for your research, it's time to sort through them and make notes for your essay. As you read your sources, write down any information that seems important to your topic. You do not need to write out full sentences from your sources—just the main points. You will save time by writing fewer words.

While you are writing your notes, you should write down the source of each piece of information. This will help you later, when you will need to find quotations or refresh your memory about a certain topic. Assign each source a code word, number, or color. When you write down a piece of information from a particular source, jot the code word or number down next to it, or make your note in the color assigned to that source.

Include the page number(s) where you got the information. When it comes time to write your essay, you will know in an instant where you got each supporting detail.

When you do not cite your sources, you are plagiarizing. *Plagiarism* is using the words or thoughts of a source without giving credit to the source.

It is a serious offense. Your teachers are trained to recognize plagiarism. Usually when someone plagiarizes, the result is a failing grade.

Plagiarism is no joke! Even a funny guy like me takes it seriously.

Sometimes it is hard to find your own words when your source's words are right in front of you. *Accidental plagiarism* happens when you do not realize you are using your source's words. You might accidentally write the same words your source used because it is so fresh in your mind. When you are writing, put your sources away to avoid accidental plagiarism.

Organizing Your Notes

As you write your notes, it can be helpful to organize them as you go. There are several ways to organize your notes. Choose a method that works well for you—there is more than one right way to take notes. Here are two methods:

1. **Note Cards**—Note cards can help you organize different types of information. If your essay has three main points, you can use different colors to stay organized. For instance, you can use three different colors of note cards—one for each main point. When you are finished making your notes, all you have to do is sort your note cards by color and you're ready for the next step.

2. **Notebooks**—Some people prefer to write their notes in notebooks. You can organize information for each of your main points a few different ways in a notebook. One is to use dividers, so there is a separate section for each main point. Another way is to use different colors of pens, one color for each main point. You might prefer to write all your notes without thinking about which main point it will support just yet. Later, you can high-light information in different colors to help you see which main point it supports.

Quoting and Paraphrasing

Once you have made all your notes, you need to find quotations from your sources to use within your essay to make your essay more believable. *Quoting* is when you use the author's words exactly. *Paraphrasing* is rewriting somebody else's ideas in your own words. You can quote and paraphrase in order to emphasize a point, to present an example, or to show a point of view.

It is important to use quotations and paraphrasing in your essay to provide context for your points. Quoting a source gives your essay credibility, or believability. You prove that other people, especially the expert who wrote the source material, verify the information in your essay. Choose quotations that show something unique or say something important about your topic. Don't use quotations for common information or basic facts.

When you are quoting in an essay, you must use quotation marks (" ") to show that you are using the exact words of someone else. When you use a quotation, you must introduce it in the sentence or attribute the source. For example, you might write:

According to the Centers for Disease Control, "carbon monoxide can cause illness and even death."

Or you might write:

"Carbon monoxide can cause illness and even death," says the Centers for Disease Control.

When you paraphrase in an essay, you do not use quotation marks because you are not using the exact words of your source. Instead, you are putting the source's unique ideas into your own words. Pretend you want to paraphrase the sentence about the effects of carbon monoxide. Here is an example:

According to the Centers for Disease Control, exposure to carbon monoxide can cause a person to get sick or even die.

Be sure not just to paraphrase and quote the ideas of others, though. Look for ways to interject your own insights and observations wherever they fit, to add voice and originality.

When you find quotations and sentences you want to paraphrase during the note-taking process, you are giving yourself a head start on writing your essay. Another way to get ahead of the game is to make an outline of your essay. Let's learn how.

Step #4: Outlines

An *outline* is a general description of the main ideas in your essay. You should make an outline before writing all kinds of essays—even in-class and test question essays. Making an outline of your essay can help you keep your ideas organized, which can save you time. While you are writing, your outline will help keep you on track—you will always know where you are in the writing process, and what is coming up next.

Let's look at an example of an outline for an essay.

Essay Prompt: Weigh the pros and cons of cell phones at school. Do you think students should be allowed to bring cell phones to school? Why or why not?

   I. Introduction

  II. Carrying a cell phone to school has some benefits.
- **A.** Students can call for help in emergency.
- **B.** Students can arrange rides if they miss the bus.
- **C.** Students can tell their parents about changes in plans.

 III. But the problems outweigh the benefits.
- **A.** Ringing cell phones can interrupt class and school activities.
- **B.** Students shouldn't be making personal calls during the school day.
- **C.** Cell phones can get damaged or stolen—costs a lot of money.

IV. Students should not be allowed to carry cell phones to school.

    A. Not enough to say students can bring cell phones but must turn them off. Someone might forget—one cell phone interruption is too many.

    B. The risk of damaged or stolen cell phones not worth the convenience.

    C. The chance of an emergency is small—students could use school phones in true emergencies anyway.

V. Conclusion

When you are finished writing your outline, read it over several times. Does it make sense? Is there any important information missing? If you aren't satisfied with the way it turned out, go back to your research material and notes to see how to fix the problem. Remember: Careful preparation makes the writing part go much more easily and smoothly.

Chapter Four

Time to Write!

Your topic has been chosen. You have done your research and taken notes. You have organized your information. Finally, it's time to start writing your essay. When you are preparing to write, make sure to set aside enough time and work in a suitable environment. If you write better on a computer, make sure to reserve a workstation at the library, or make sure your little brother knows you will be on your home computer for a while—no interruptions. Other people prefer to write with pen and paper. Keep lots of fresh paper and pens or pencils close by. Find a quiet place to begin writing and get started!

Parts of an Essay

An essay has three parts: the *introduction*, the *body*, and the *conclusion*. Each part serves a specific purpose. The introduction tells your reader what topic you will be writing about, and it includes the thesis statement. The body paragraphs include the supporting details. The conclusion summarizes the most important parts of the essay and leaves the reader with a clear understanding of the topic. In this chapter, you will learn how to write each part of an essay.

Introduction Paragraph

The introduction tells your reader what you are writing about. It gets the reader ready for the information in the essay. An effective introduction is an important part of a successful essay. It allows your reader to follow the supporting details in your body paragraphs better,

I prefer the computer.

I'm a pencil guy, myself!

which will lead to a better overall understanding of your essay. It is also a chance to make a good first impression. If your introduction is strong, you will gain credibility.

An introduction usually starts with a general statement about your topic. It is a place to show where your topic fits into the world and why it is an important topic to be writing about. For example, if you are writing an essay about the effects of cigarette smoking, your first sentence might be:

According to the Centers for Disease Control, smoking cigarettes leads to more deaths every year than any other cause.

The next sentence or two in your introduction should give more details about your topic:

Even though smoking is so deadly, it is still too easy for teens to buy cigarettes illegally.

The last sentence in your introduction paragraph is usually the thesis statement. As you have learned, the thesis statement tells your reader exactly what you will show in your essay:

In order to stop teens from smoking, stores that sell cigarettes must try harder to prevent the illegal sale of cigarettes.

Body Paragraphs

After the introduction paragraph, it's time for the body paragraphs of your essay. When you learned about thesis statements, you learned that they include two or three main points that you will prove in your essay.

Each of these main points will have a body paragraph in your essay. Each body paragraph will contain facts and examples that support the main point. Let's look at an example. If your thesis statement is, "Technology has given people a better life by improving medical care, adding convenience, and increasing jobs," then you will have three body paragraphs.

One body paragraph will show how technology has improved medical care. You might discuss ways that technology has improved medical tools, how doctors use computers to find information quickly, and how people use the Internet to learn how to stay healthy.

Your next body paragraph will give examples of how technology has made life more convenient. You could talk about using cell phones in emergencies and how computers make the checkout lines at the store go more quickly.

Your last body paragraph will discuss how technology has increased the number of jobs. Your essay could discuss the people who build computers and other technical equipment, like telephones, televisions, and cars. You could talk about how most companies hire people to take care of their computers and build their Web sites.

Each body paragraph will start with a sentence that tells the reader what main point you will prove within it. This is called the topic sentence. The middle sentences in your paragraph will contain the facts and details that prove your main point. The last sentence in a body paragraph will summarize your main point.

Conclusion Paragraph

The last paragraph of your essay is the conclusion. The conclusion will summarize your essay. Remember not to introduce any new information during the conclusion. In the first sentence in your conclusion paragraph, you will restate your thesis. The other sentences summarize your main points, show what you learned from writing the paper, or give a vision for the future. A good conclusion will leave your reader with a clear understanding of the points in your essay. Let's look at an example of a conclusion paragraph.

In order to become an excellent soccer player, athletes must be disciplined about practice to increase the physical skills needed to be a good player. Playing soccer is a lot of hard work, and sometimes it can be tough to find time to get better. But the payoff is worth it as the crowd rises to their feet and yells "Score!" as the ball flies past the goalie.

Now that you know what is included within each section of an essay, it's time to practice it yourself. Time for the rough draft!

Step #5: Rough Draft

The first step in crafting an effective essay is to write the rough draft. The rough draft is the first try at the final essay you will turn in. You will be reworking and rewriting this draft, so it does not have to be perfect. When you are writing the rough draft, look at the big picture. Focus on the main points and getting your ideas on paper in the most logical way possible.

When you begin writing, work from your outline, writing each section based on the ideas you need to develop. You will also write from the notes you took during your research. If you are having trouble, try writing a sticky note for each of the facts in your research. On a poster board, bulletin board, or just your wall or desk, arrange the sticky notes in order, based on your outline. If you get "stuck" on an idea while writing your rough draft, you can just glance at your wall of facts to help clear up any confusion.

Just don't get stuck on your sticky notes!

When you have written down all the information you want to include, your rough draft is done. The next step is to make changes that will make your essay even better.

Chapter Five

Making It Even Better

N ow it's time to revise, edit, and proofread your work. *Revising* your essay means making changes to the content. You might find that two of your sentences could be combined into one sentence. Maybe you decide that you want to move one main point to the end. Perhaps you have repeated an idea unnecessarily or left out a key fact. *Editing* your essay means making sure your sentences are written clearly and make sense to your audience. *Proofreading* is looking for mistakes in spelling, grammar, and punctuation.

Every first draft of an essay needs to be revised, edited, and proofread, even if you think at first that it is perfect. In order for your essay to be effective and credible, it must be free of mistakes. Let's learn all about how to make your essay better.

Step #6: Revising, Editing, and Proofreading

Revising

The first step of the process is to revise your work. To revise literally means to "re-see." When you revise your essay, you are focusing on the content rather than mechanical issues like spelling, grammar, and punctuation.

So what exactly should you look at while you are revising? Make sure your essay has a clear introduction and conclusion. Make sure the body paragraphs support your thesis. Look to see if the sentences make sense. You might find that one of the sentences needs to be more descriptive and clear. Another sentence might be unneeded, and you can take it out. One of your ideas might need more development. Or perhaps you decide that your paragraphs seem out of order.

A good way to approach the revision process is to pretend

This essay needs a tune-up. Time to revise!

you know nothing about the topic. This can be tough, since you have been researching and studying the topic for some time. Try to clear your mind before you begin revising. If you are having trouble, ask a parent, friend, or classmate to read it for you and comment on which parts don't make sense or need more development.

Editing

The next step is to edit your essay. Editing is making sure your writing is clear, makes sense, and is appropriate for your audience. Read each sentence and paragraph and ask yourself, Will the audience understand it? Is there a better way to phrase the sentence or paragraph? Have you chosen the best words that show what you are trying to say? If you think there might be a better word than the one you have used, look it up in a thesaurus. Just be sure not to "overdose" on big, flowery words!

Proofreading

Last of all, you need to proofread—or proof— your essay. Proofreading is correcting errors and inconsistencies in mechanics, such as spelling, grammar, punctuation, and language. Don't worry, every writer makes mistakes in the rough draft. You are now on a mission—find those mistakes and force them out of your essay!

Read your essay several times and look for any mistakes you have made. What kinds of mistakes should you look for?

- **spelling**—Is every word spelled correctly? If you aren't sure whether a word is spelled correctly, look it up in the dictionary.

- **grammar**—Are your sentences grammatically correct? If you aren't sure, do some research or ask a parent, friend, or teacher for help.

- **punctuation**—Do you use periods, commas, and other punctuation marks correctly?

Once you are sure your essay does not contain any mistakes, read it one more time so you are confident that it is the best it can be. Read it out loud if you can.

When to Revise, Edit, and Proof

One of your most important strategies is timing. For revising, editing, and proofing to be most effective, you should allow your finished rough draft to sit untouched for a while. This will allow you to return to it with a fresh mind and fresh eyes. In order to leave enough time for revising and editing, you must be sure to plan ahead and pace yourself.

Of course, for an in-class essay,

Be wise—revise!

Don't forget it—gotta edit!

you won't be able to put the essay aside for a day or two, and you won't be able to show it to anyone else for their input. Don't worry, there are strategies you can use during in-class essays as well. First, make sure to leave time after writing your essay for editing, revising, and proofing. If you have time, read your work twice. The first time you read your essay, make sure your ideas are clear and check to see if there are any words or sentences that can be deleted. Check that all of your words are precise and are used correctly. The second time you read your essay, look for errors in spelling, grammar, and punctuation.

Computer Editing Tools

Correct spelling and grammar are very important. If you are using a word-processing program to write your essay, you probably have access to the program's spell-checker and grammar checker. These tools can help sometimes, but both the spell-checker and the grammar checker can make mistakes, so you can't rely on them alone. It is a good idea to ask another person to read your essay and look for anything the spell-checker and grammar checker might have missed.

Evaluating

As you revise, edit and proofread, evaluate how well your essay fulfills the requirements for the essay assignment. Some teachers provide their students with a *rubric*—a list of guidelines that tell what the teacher is looking for in an assignment and, sometimes, how it will be graded. If your teacher has not given you a rubric, use a checklist like the one below and mark off everything you have done in your essay. If anything is not checked, ask yourself how you can make it better! When you can check each column with a "yes," you have an effective essay!

Does your essay have . . .	Yes	No
Clear choice of topic	☐	☐
Strong introduction	☐	☐
Solid thesis statement	☐	☐
Paragraphs well organized	☐	☐
Each paragraph proves a point in the thesis	☐	☐
Strong conclusion	☐	☐
Content easy to understand	☐	☐
Descriptive words	☐	☐
Good transition words	☐	☐
Correct capitalization	☐	☐
Proper grammar	☐	☐
Correct punctuation	☐	☐
Correct spelling	☐	☐

Chapter Six

Presenting It

You're almost done. Once your essay has been written, revised, and edited, it's time to submit your final draft. Presenting a clean, good-looking essay is the final step in the essay writing process.

Step #7: Preparing the Final Draft

Format

Your essay should be typed in an easy-to-read format.

When you type your essay, make sure it is easy to read. Double-space your essay, use a standard font like Times New Roman or Arial, and use a large enough font (10 or 12 point). If you are not sure how to double-space or change the font, ask your librarian or a friend for help. Make sure to find out whether your teacher has other requirements for typed essays, such as margin size, numbering the pages, what font to use, and where to put your name and class information.

When you think that you are ready to turn in your final draft, give it one last look. Does it look good? Have you done everything you can to make it your very best work? When you have answered yes to these questions, it's time to hand it in.

Be sure to save your final draft first then print it out.

Hurray! You've written an essay!

Get Feedback

Many times, you will have the opportunity to see what comments your audience has about your essay. You can have a friend or parent read your essay and give you feedback, and often your teacher will make comments while grading the essay. Use this opportunity to look for ways to improve your essay writing skills. Read your teacher's comments

Appearance counts! Don't turn in a sloppy essay!

carefully. If you have any questions about your essay or the comments your teacher has made, now is the time to ask. Remember, you will write many essays in your lifetime, and now is the best time to learn as much as you can about how to do it well.

Other Ways to Present Your Essay

Your essay is written. You've handed it in. You're really proud of the way it turned out, and you would like to share your ideas and research with even more people. Well, don't let your essay hide in a drawer

'Zine it!

'Zine is short for magazine. It is a booklet that you publish yourself. A 'zine is an easy to make booklet that contains, well, just about anything you want.

How can you turn your essay into a 'zine? Try drawing a cartoon, or find pictures to illustrate your essay. Make a title page (don't forget to list your name as the author) and staple the pages together to make a booklet.

You can publish every essay you write in a new issue of your 'zine, or team up with your classmates to make a group 'zine project. Save your dimes and make copies of your 'zine, then (with your teacher's permission) pass them out to your friends, family members, classmates, and teachers, or publish your 'zine online.

somewhere! You can reach an even wider audience by posting your essay on the Internet, sending it to the editor of your local newspaper, or presenting it as a speech. Think about who might be interested in your topic and contact that person or organization. Your essay could make a difference in your school, your community, or even the world.

Hurray for Essays!

You've achieved something significant by writing an essay: You have shared your ideas with the world. And hopefully you've had some fun along the way. Next time your teacher says, "Write an essay ..." what will you say?

"Hurray! I get to write an essay!"

A Sample Student Essay

Adam has been assigned a take-home essay for English class. First, he reads the prompt:

Describe an event in your life that changed you in some way and tell why this experience was important to you.

Adam realizes that this assignment is for a narrative essay. Once he feels that he understands what the teacher is looking for, Adam thinks about some topic ideas. He decides to write about his passion—art. He jots down a few notes and comes up with his main point:

Notes:
art—from doodling to oil paints, when did I first become serious about it? . . . when I was stuck in bed, Aunt Julie's gift, learned to turn a bad situation into a good one.

Main point:
A time that seemed at first to be horrible and unfair turned out to be a blessing because I discovered my talent for painting.

Now it's time to outline. Here's what Adam comes up with:

Adam's essay outline

I. Introduction

When I was seven, I was stuck in bed with a broken ankle and bad cold. I thought it was the worst time of my life but it became one of the best.

II. Things were looking bad

    A. Was trapped, bored, and lonely

    B. Aunt Julie brought me a present

    C. I didn't believe anything could make me feel better

III. I discovered painting

    A. Opened the box and found quality art materials

    B. Painted my cast

    C. Loved it!!! Became an artist

IV. How I used that experience afterward

    A. Kept painting

    B. Grew as an artist

    C. Exhibited my paintings

V. Conclusion

    The lesson of Aunt Julie's gift: Good things can come from bad times

Adam then puts all of his ideas together, and, after revising, editing, and proofing, comes up with this final essay.

An Unexpected Gift

by Adam Jackson

It was going to be the worst weekend of my life. I just knew it. I was seven years old, summer vacation had just begun, and the whole world was out enjoying the sunshine and freedom. Except me—I was stuck in bed. I had broken my ankle playing soccer on a rainy soccer field and had a plaster cast on my foot and leg. To make matters worse, I also had come down with a bad cold. I wasn't allowed out of bed, and my friends weren't allowed to visit my bedroom in case I was contagious. At first I was miserable, but then an amazing thing happened, something so wonderful it changed my life.

Aunt Julie stopped in to see me. She said that she never caught colds and that she knew I would be lonely and might need cheering up. Then she handed me a little box. I told her "thank you." What I really wanted to say was, "I'm trapped and lonely and uncomfortable and totally BUMMED OUT!" I was stuck staring at four walls and lame TV (no cable) during vacation, and she thought a little box would magically make things better? Ha! To be polite, I opened the gift. It was a set of paints. Aunt Julie gave me a kiss, told me to have fun, and left.

I looked over the little pots of colors. I took out the two paintbrushes. They were very good quality art supplies. Before this, I'd never used such fancy art materials. Sure, I'd always liked the 64-crayon box and smooshy fingerpaints. I doodled all the time on scrap paper and in my school notebooks. But this was grown-up stuff! I wanted to use it right away.

Then I realized I had no paper. What could I paint? My leg cast, of course! I spent the whole afternoon decorating my cast. I painted animals and monsters and funky designs. I had a blast. I loved mixing colors, creating images, even the smell of the paint. Time zoomed by. I wasn't depressed anymore. I was an ARTIST!

In the six years since a leg cast became my first canvas, barely a day has gone by that I haven't picked up a paintbrush. I've taken painting classes at the art museum, read about famous painters, and even had my artwork shown at local exhibits!

I still have bad days (and weekends) sometimes, of course. I am a teenager, and I know life can't be perfect. But I can always look back to the day Aunt Julie gave me a small gift to cheer me up and remember that good things can come from bad times. And maybe someday I can pass along that gift to someone else.

Glossary

body—The section between the introduction and conclusion that develops the main idea.

conclusion—The end of a piece of writing.

draft—A version of a piece of writing.

edit—To improve your work by making sure your writing is clear and makes sense.

expository essay—An essay that explains something in detail.

introduction—The beginning of a piece of writing.

narrative essay—An essay about a personal experience.

paraphrase—To put someone else's words into your words.

persuasive essay—An essay that tries to convince your readers to believe the same thing you do about a subject.

plagiarize—To use someone else's words or ideas without giving them credit.

proofread—To make sure your work is mistake-free.

prompt—A statement that tells you what to write about.

quote—To use someone else's words directly.

revise—To make changes in the content of a piece of writing.

rubric—The guidelines against which your piece of writing will be evaluated.

thesis statement—The sentence in your essay that tells what your essay is about.

topic—The main idea or subject.

Further Reading

Books

Northey, Margot, and MiKibbin, Joan. *Making Sense: A Student's Guide To Research and Writing.* Don Mills, Ont: Oxford University Press, 2005.

Orr, Tamra. *Extraordinary Essays.* New York: Scholastic Press, 2005.

Wilson, Laura. *Write The SAT Essay Right!: Ten Secrets To Add 100 Points To Your Score.* Florida: Maupin House, 2010.

Internet Addresses

The Owl Purdue Online Writing Lab; Essay Writing
<http://owl.english.purdue.edu/owl/resource/685/01/>

How to Write an Essay
<http://kimberlychapman.com/essay/essay.html>

Index

A

accidental plagiarism, 35

B

body paragraph, 41, 42–44

C

cause-and-effect essay, 14, 17–18
college application essay, 9, 18–19, 24–25
compare-and-contrast essay, 14, 15–17
computer editing tools, 50
conclusion paragraph, 41, 44

E

editing, 46, 48, 49–50
essay, definition of, 6–9
essay prompts, 8, 27–28
essay questions, 20–22
essay test, 19–23
essay topic, 27–30
expository essay, 10, 14–18

F

final draft, 52–55
feedback on, 53–54
format, 52–53
presenting, 54–55

I

in-class essay, 19–23
Internet research, 32–34
introduction paragraph, 41–42

L

library research, 31–32

N

narrative essay, 10–11
notebooks, 35–36
note cards, 35
note-taking, 34–36

O

outline, 38–39

P

paraphrasing, 36–37
persuasive essay, 10, 11–14
plagiarism, 34–35
position paper, 13–14
problem/solution essay, 12–13

process paper, 14–15
prompts, 8, 27–28
proofreading, 46, 48–50

Q

quotations, 36–37

R

research material, 31–34
revising, 46, 47–48, 49–50
rough draft, 44–45
rubric, 50–51

S

sample essay, 57–60
SATs, 19–20
standardized tests, 19–20
studying, 31

T

take-home essay, 18, 23–24, 31
thesis statement, 30–31, 41, 42
topic, 27–30

Z

'zine, 55